Celebrating

Valentine's Day

By: Shelly Nielsen

Illustrated by: Marie-Claude Monchaux

Published by Abdo & Daughters, 4940 Viking Drive, Suite 622, Edina, Minnesota 55435.

Library bound edition distributed by Rockbottom Books, Pentagon Tower, P.O. Box 36036, Minneapolis, Minnesota 55435.

Printed in the United States.

Illustrations by Marie-Claude Monchaux.

Edited by Julie Berg

Library of Congress Cataloging-in-Publication Data
Nielsen, Shelly, 1958-
      Valentine's Day / Shelly Nielsen.
         p. cm. -- (Holiday Celebrations)
      Summary: Rhyming text introduces aspects of this holiday which falls on February 14.
      ISBN 1-56239-703-6
      1. Valentine's Day--Juvenile literature. [1.Valentine's Day.] I. Title.II. Series: Nielsen, Shelly, 1958-
      Holiday celebrations.
    GT4925.N54 1996
    394.2'61--dc20
                                          96-12759
                                             CIP
                                             AC

Celebrating

Valentine's Day

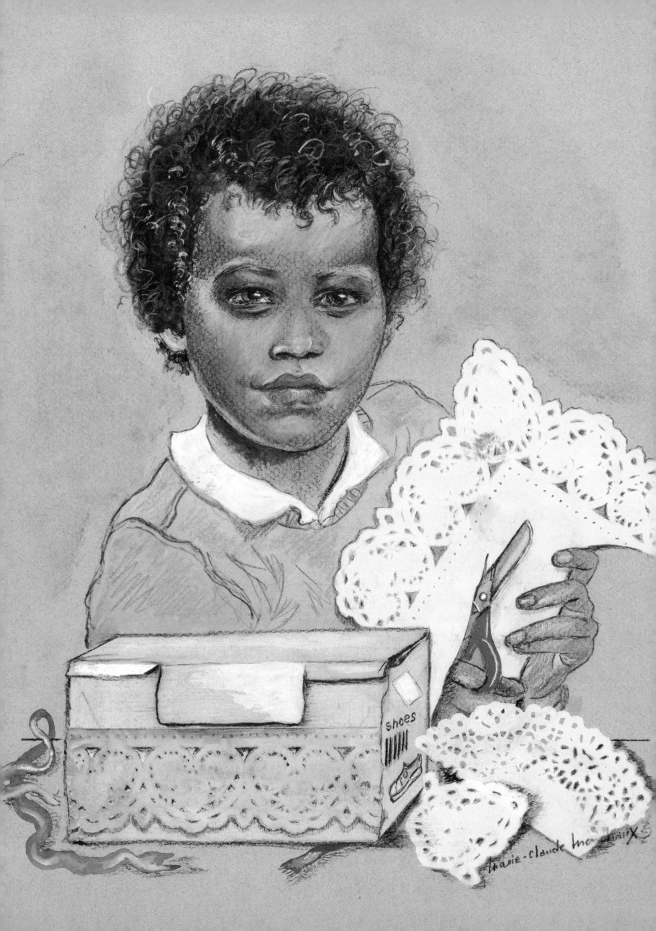

My Valentine Box

It was just a shoe box
ugly and plain.
But I wrapped it in paper,
trimmed it with lace,
added a doily,
and some cellophane tape.
Hmmm…
Something was missing.
So I cut a slot—
long and slender,
right through the top.
It's ready for school now,
waiting by the door.
Tomorrow it will hold valentines,
a million…or more!

Cookies, Please

Sugar, flour, butter.
Mix it in a bowl.
Pat it,
roll it,
bake it.
I love heart cookies so!
Sparkly with sugar,
crispy on your teeth,
sugar cookies for Valentine's Day
are good enough to eat!

Message to a Friend

It was just a simple valentine,
sent a day ago.
I picked it out
with kindly thoughts
for someone that I know.

"To my pal Meg from Annie,"
I wrote with careful hand.
What a good way to say "Happy Valentine's Day"
and "You're a special friend!"

Old-Fashioned Valentines

Under the bed, next to the boxes of clothes,
Grandma keeps valentines from long ago.
We sit together and open the box.
The cards smell wonderful—
of secrets and dust.
Carefully, carefully...I touch each one
trying to imagine Grandmother young.
Now I'm saving my valentines, too,
for when my grandchildren ask,
"Can we look at cards with you?"

For My Pet

Here's a mushy, gushy valentine
for my pooch;
delivered with a dog cookie,
a hug, and a muzzle smooch!

Paper Hearts

Paper hearts
through the house;
I cut them out
by myself.
Big ones,
little ones,
sweet as can be...
They're in the beds
on the TV,
in the cupboards,
in the drawers,
on the table,
on the floor.
Valentine's Day is the time of year
when paper hearts appear!

School Party Time

Hurry! Hurry! Hand your cards out fast!
There's one for everyone in the class.
The envelopes have a name on each,
and the valentines inside are funny or sweet.
Some have cartoons to make you laugh,
drawings of elephants, mice, giraffes,
hearts and flowers, kittens and lace...
Valentines put smiles on every face.

To My Teacher

What's behind me?
A surprise
for my teacher,
kind and wise.
Is it diamonds?
A rose bunch?
Chocolates
to munch?
Some treasure
from a store shelf?
No,
a beautiful valentine
I made myself.

VALENTINE'S DAY

Conversation Hearts

VALENTINE LOVE
CUTIE PIE
DREAM OF ME
MY DELIGHT
CAN'T WAIT
GIVE A SQUEEZE
BE MINE
PRETTY PLEASE
SIGH!

Mystery Valentine

I opened my desk, took a look,
and found a secret valentine
under papers and books.
No name was signed,
just "Your secret pal."
Who sent it?
No one will tell.
I can't stand it!
Was it Katie? Jo? Heather?
Still ...
It's nice to have a secret admirer.

Chocolate Surprise

Valentine's Day brings chocolates
nestled in a box,
sitting in their ruffly papers;
I could eat them nonstop.
Caramels are delicious.
Vanilla creams are tops.
Bonbons, truffles, minty squares—
I just can't get enough.
The trouble is, you can never tell
what you'll get until you bite.
You might get coconut or cherry-filled
or some awful nut delight.
And once you bite,
you can't put it back;
adults don't think that's keen.
So I'm sure glad
there's no such flavors as bug or lima bean!

A Valentine's Day Kiss

My best gift for Mommy
didn't come in a box.
It wasn't wrapped in paper
with a bow on top.
I didn't buy it at a store
or fix it in a dish.
I just wrapped my arms around Mom
and gave her a Valentine kiss.